THIS BOOK BELONGS TO:

_____

THIS BOOK IS DEDICATED TO FIREFIGHTERS AND FUTURE FIREFIGHTERS.

Copyright © 2024 Grow Grit Press LLC. All rights reserved. No part of this book may be reproduced in any form without permission in writing from the publisher. Please send bulk order requests to info@ninjalifehacks.tv

Paperback ISBN: 978-1-63731-945-1
Hardcover ISBN: 978-1-63731-947-5
eBook ISBN: 978-1-63731-946-8

Printed and bound in the USA.
NinjaLifeHacks.tv

Ninja Life Hacks®
by Mary Nhin

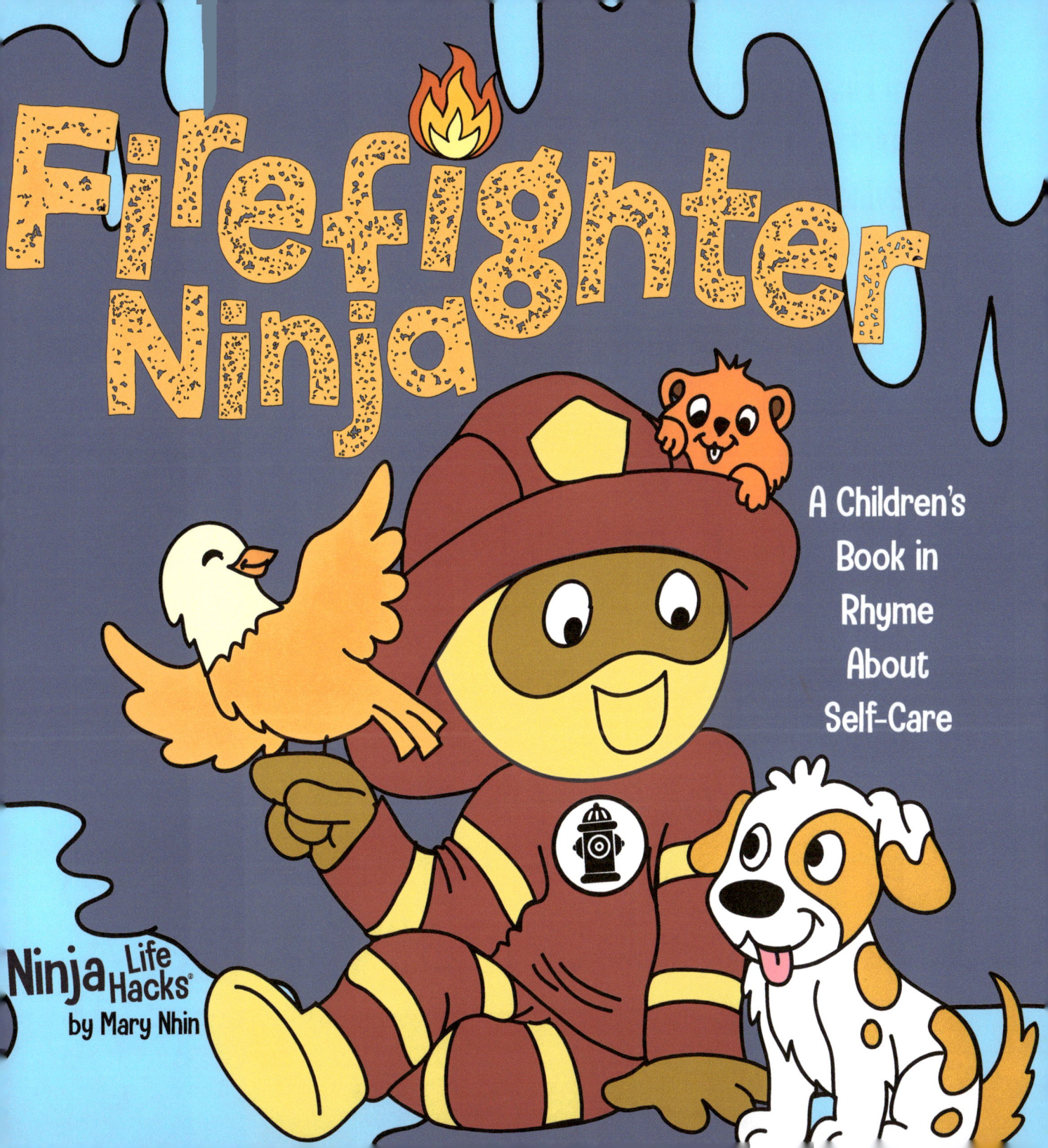

One day, the fire alarm
Went off and rang loud,
A fire blazed
With a smoky cloud.

My friends came over,
Shaking their heads.
"You need to rest,"
Is what they said.

I love to hear from my readers. Email me your feedback or thoughts on what my next story should be at info@ninjalifehacks.tv

Yours truly, Mary

 @marynhin   @GrowGrit   #NinjaLifeHacks

 Mary Nhin   Ninja Life Hacks

 Ninja Life Hacks

 @officialninjalifehacks

Continue the learning with fun social, emotional worksheets and printables at ninjalifehacks.tv

Firefighter Ninja Tower Challenge

Objective: Build a tower that can withstand a "fire" (wind or vibrations) using simple materials.

Supplies needed:

 Spaghetti noodles

 Marshmallows or clay (for connectors)

 Paper cups

 Tape

 Scissors

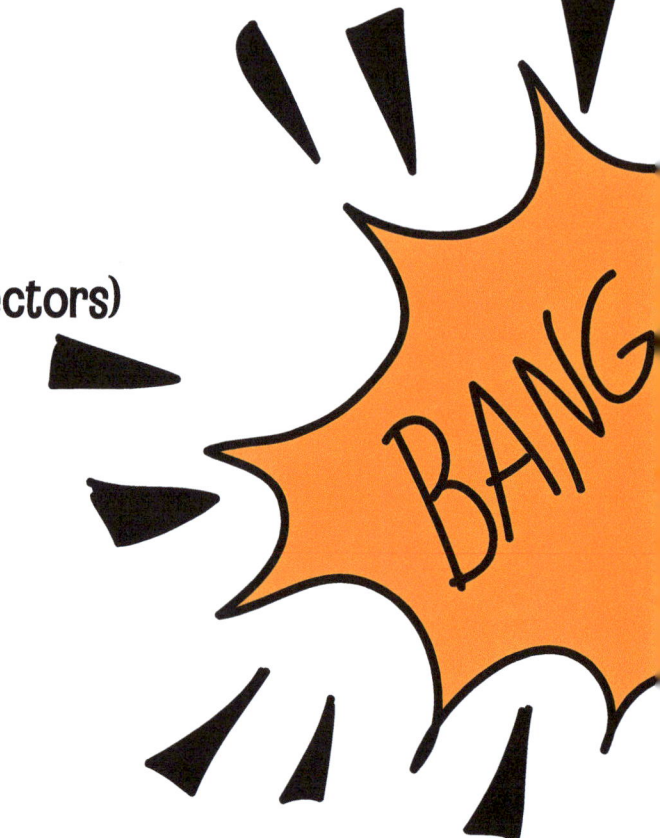

Instructions:

1. **Build the Tower:**
   🔥 Give each group a set of spaghetti noodles and marshmallows or clay.
   🔥 Challenge them to build the tallest and most stable tower using these materials. The tower should be able to hold a paper cup on top.

2. **Test the Stability:**
   🔥 Create a "fire" simulation by gently blowing on the tower or placing it on a vibrating surface (like a piece of cardboard that can be gently tapped).

3. **Evaluate and Improve:**
   🔥 Discuss which designs were the most stable and why. Allow time for adjustments and re-testing.

www.ingramcontent.com/pod-product-compliance
Lightning Source LLC
Chambersburg PA
CBHW041713160426
43209CB00018B/1825